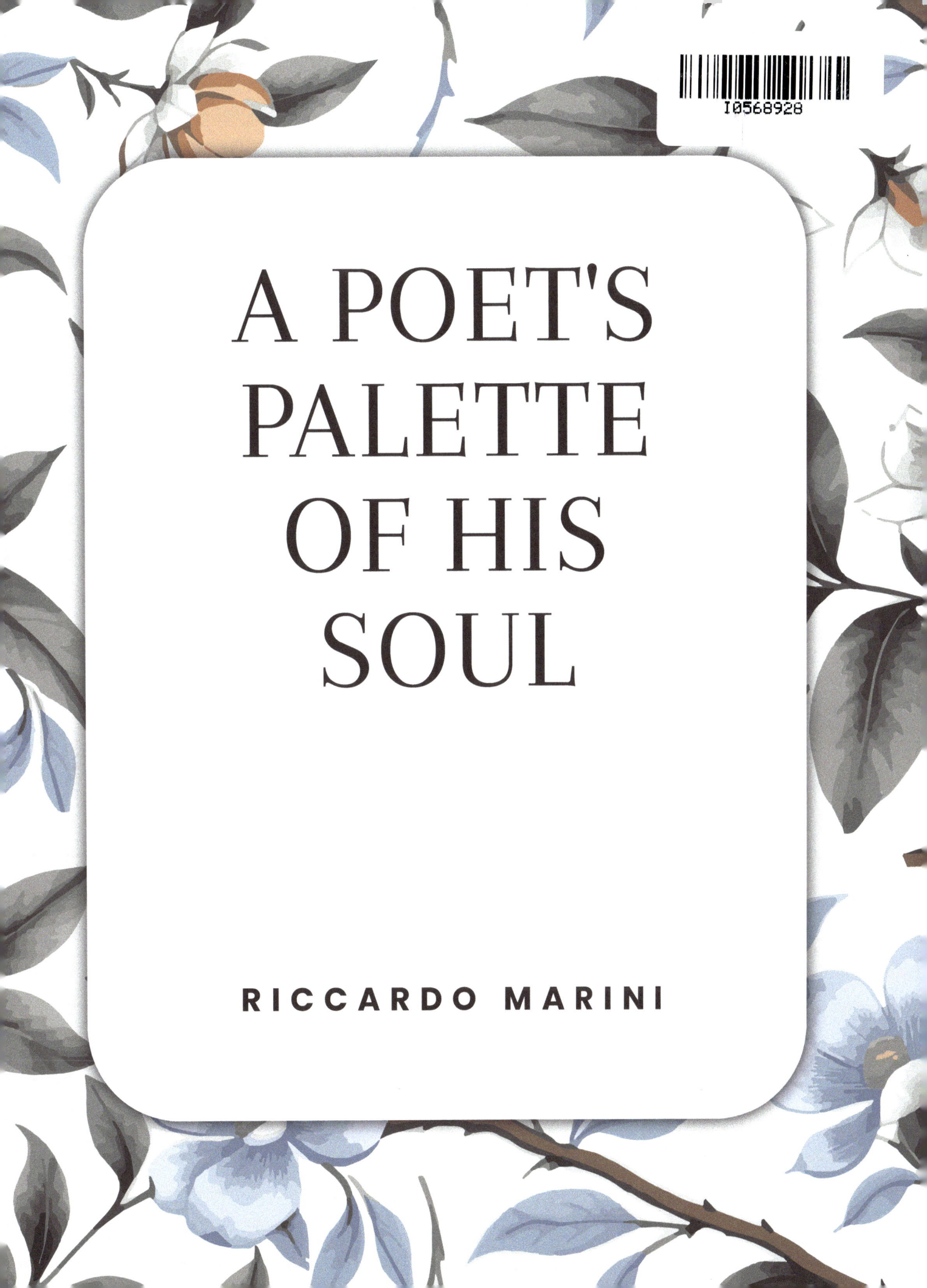

A POET'S PALETTE OF HIS SOUL

RICCARDO MARINI

A Palette of Artistic Poetry Verse and Color
Thoughts that will inspire,

Make you laugh,

Make you ponder,

Make you tear,

Make you love,

Make you live

Edited by: Riccardo Marini and Virginia Brancaccio

Poetry by: Riccardo Marini

Illustration Artwork by: Virginia Brancaccio

Cover design by: Book Publishing Company

Library In Congress Catalogue # 2025917692

Printed In the United States of America

JENRICH PUBLISHING
WORDS OF WISDOM

Riccardo Marini
ISBN: 978-1-969368-10-3

9 781969 368103

Table of Contents

Dedication

To all the people I have written about
And all those that will read my book
And all those that have inspired me
And all those that have loved me,
especially Virginia Brancaccio

"Imagined for You"

By Riccardo Marini - 2024

As the winds ever-change the beauty of the hills

With tranquility I stand in these beautiful fields

Each flower brushed with care

By dancing butterflies Caressing each petal

As if it was the last chance

To a lifetime romance

I hear the whispers of summer breezes

As they say, a prayer of worship

Across the horizon I see a dance

Of gentle sprinkles of sunshine rain

Placing me in a solitude trance

A fragile world painted in shades of green and blue

We need to love and nurture

for our children's future

While I Create a Palette of Artistic

Poetry Imagined for you.

"Love In-a-Mist"

By Riccardo Marini - 2024
We were in our teens
When I remember our first kiss
What I remember most
How you closed your eyes
With love-in-a-mist

We walked to school
Holding hands
As I carried your books
I admired your looks.

Then one day
As you stood against the tree
I looked in your eyes
And asked, would you marry me?

I leaned over to give you a kiss
What I remember most

How you closed your eyes
With love-in-a-mist
On our wedding day
At our special dance
We kissed and kissed

What I remember most
How you closed your eyes
With love-in-a-mist.

And on our honeymoon
We danced all night
Made love from dusk to dawn

I held you tight
As we kissed by fireplace light
Ambers burned

The seasons came and went
Jobs and work soon arrived
Followed by

Cars, homes, kids and fights

Vacations, birthdays, graduations
Showers, weddings and celebrations
Life's accelerations

The spring flowers and endless summers
The falling leaves' Falls,
And Winter winds' snow

The snowmen and angels
Grandkids and toys
The fun, laughter
And all the joys

The time has passed
I can tell by the empty hourglass
With each grain of sand
Slipping through our aching, fragile hands

The top once filled with promise

And an empty bottom awaited
Now with a few grains left
With our breaths abated.

We lay next to each other
Watching a vintage movie
Holding hands, I kiss you goodnight

What I remember most
With a tear and love-in-a-mist.
How you closed your eyes for the last time
And never kiss again

Love-in-a-Mist holds deep symbolism and represents several qualities and emotions. Its delicate and intricate flowers symbolize love, affection, and mystery.

Cherché

"On Angel Wings"

By Riccardo Marini - 2024
I was flying, but couldn't land
Like a bird without feet
I was flying asleep.

Too young to understand
Life has the upper hand
I, just an ordinary man
Reaching for cherché

Flying and flying above
Flying and flying above
I never stopped, I never stopped.

Cherché, cherché
With broken wings
And broken heart
With obscured vision
Like a blind man in the dark

Without a destination
Without a plan
Mentally fatigued

How could I ever land
Afterall, I had no feet
My fate a pool of quicksand

Through wind, rain and storm
I asked, where did I belong?
Like a bird without feet
I was flying asleep

'Till you came along, 'till you came along
You gave me guidance
You gave me strength
As I rested on your wings, as I rested on your wings

We soared and soared and soared
We flew above the heavens
And landed on your Angel Wings

trust
betrayal
What kind
of friend
would be"?
FORGOTTEEN
GLOOM

What Kind of Friend Would You Be?

By Riccardo Marini - 2024

If you were my dream friend
What would I find at the end?

Would I find you on a dusty, boring un-swept corner room
Or, perhaps on my mind's forgotten shelf of forgotten gloom?

Would I find you in bright lights performing to a crowd
Without me standing alongside the stage?

Would you be endowed?
With an imagination that creates fireworks when you speak.

Or would you have fallen
Into a molded basement suitcase lying around all by yourself?

Would you carry secrets to my grave?
Or would you share them to my face?

Would your message be distracting of emotion?
Sadly, void of grace?
Or would it be cheerfully nice? Which I could share

Would you fabricate creating a thrill for my pleasure?
Or would you not care how I felt to any measure?

Would you be my soul's confidant?
Or, happy to observe from a distance
My anxiety, my struggles that you might mitigate

Would you examine the frightful thoughts I've buried deeply
In the valleys of my mind?
And build me a staircase to help bring them to the surface
To deal with my sublime?

Would your insightful poetic writings make me feel like a bird in flight?
Or would your character display deceit,
Would you hide yourself if I came calling for an important task
In need in the middle of night

Would you lie under our oath?
Would you steal the gold from my teeth?

Would you watch me kneel in grief
Crying a river of tears beneath my feet

Or would you build a dam to hold back the flood
So, some day you will open the gates
With pleasure and watch me drown

Or would you enter my soul With a bucket and mop
and take as long as it would take To dry it all up?

And if you could gift yourself to anyone in the world,
Who would you choose?
Me or someone else?

Could you bleed every last drop
To give to me?
And no-one else?

Could you read me a love story
Holding my hand as I fell asleep
Cause I would like to know
What kind of friend would you be?

My Central Park

By Riccardo Marini - 2024

Horse drawn carriage tours in the park

Moon scape tapestry sky lit stars

A midnight ride in the dark

The morning song of a singing Lark

All found in the backyard of my home

My Central Park

Artist paintings on the pedestrian mall

Cascading fountains misting us all

Built in stone the Grand Castle stands

Booklets, bracelets, trinkets and fables

Sold everywhere at vendor's tables

Squirrels, chipmunks and baby fawns

Strollers and picnic baskets

On the Great Green Lawn

Blooming umbrellas of elms, oaks and cherry
blossoms
The chitter chatter of stories and friendly gossips
Pecking pigeons gathering to mingle and meet
Row boats floating along dancing swans, beak to beak

Romantic dinners at the Boat House Café
Sipping champagne at the Oak Bar on a first date
A Sunday brunch at Tavern on the Green

Cloud watching teenagers
Having childhood daylight dreams
Reading a book on sun-soaked rocks
Picking a three-leave clover changing your luck

The ballet of traffic,
Of horns, bikers and joggers
Underneath canopies of Rainbow showers

Bench kissing sweetheart lovers
Spring strolling through Strawberry Fields
You can hear the tune in the breeze
Singing "Imagine" vivid and real

Summer concerts starring Simon, Garfunkel and
Billy Joel
A backdrop of blushing trees, falling leaves of the fall
Children playing, riding the giant Carousel
At noon the subtle chimes of St Patrick's Bell

Seasons pass and a changing landscape
Into a winter wonderland wrapped in ribbons
Of Red Green and White

Skaters pirouetting on a frozen Pond
A snow-white blanket covering its sacred ground
A Museum, a Zoo and a Planetarium too
Snowflakes glistening on Christmas Tree lights
Making dreams come true

On bridges and pathways made of cobble stone
Leading to a magical place
Dear to my heart
Home sweet Home
My Central Park

75

By Riccardo Marini - 2024
You haven't changed at 75,
Time may have weaved a subtle line.
I can see it in your eyes,
Your beauty, it still shines.

You haven't changed at 75,
I can feel it when we touch,
You're just as soft and kind

You haven't changed at 75,
Your heart's warmth, ever pure,
Guiding us through life's changes
with every beat and reason

I can still see the waves in your beautiful hair,
Each strand tells a tale we arranged,
Of our love's journey, bold and brave.

For the last 25 years
You have been my songbird.
Perched upon a branch,
in the morning's embrace

Unleashing its song,
with effortless grace.
Your words dance in the breeze,

A symphony so rare,
With echoes of wonder,
filling the air.

And on your 75th year embrace,
Our love, eternal, never dies.
Keep singing my songbird your grace,
You're a beacon and a companion to all

Sing your melody, sing through all the seasons
For every note we hear
It's filled with Virginia's song of solace and cheer

The King Majesty, Sir Richard Bloom

By Riccardo Marini - 2024

In the autumn of life
At a bold eighty, filled with vigor presumed
There stands a man named Sir Richard Bloom

Waving like a reed in the breeze
He can make you feel at ease
In his eyes, the fire of a tiger
Is what people see

The King Majesty sits on his throne
A Master of Ceremonies So, he's been known
A conductor of cheer
He orchestrates laughter to the ear
He can bring you to joyful tears

With wit and humor, his stage is vast
A maestro of mirth

Making moments last and last

In the spotlight he shares a beacon of glee
A charmer of crowds, for all to see

A Fred Astaire look-alike
Filled with glamour and poise
A charmer, a lover
At a moment's notice he's overjoyed

But in the quiet corners
Where shadows may creep
His cat Mercedes in slumber, finds her keep

McAllen Scotch, his favored libation
In a crystal glass a large cube awaits
A toast to life's celebration
He's always ready to make

You can tell when he's in a room
A scent of Jaipur by Boucheronc

Fills his golden plume

His elegance and grace

In every step he makes

Sir Richard you're forever enshrined with angels of like and kind

Daily, he tends to his silvering hair

Each strand combed with meticulous care

A long time ago it was painted brownish red

Now a golden silver fox as he lays his head

On the pillow each night he dreams

Of culinary delights

Of a medium rare tomahawk steak

Grilled to perfection in every single bite

At times obsessed with gadgetry

The digital embrace makes his personal space

Computer screens and cell phones Is his technological place

A Public Speaker A passion he unveils

Words that resonate Like poetic tales.

The crowds he entertains
Laugh till they cry
They dance and dance, through the midnight skies

Yet, in moments of solitude
Grumpy he may be and quietly shy
A symphony of emotions

A complex swirling sea
His ocean swirls and swirls
His mind spins and spins
Of UFO visions to the tune of "Begin the Beguine"

But beneath the surface of high esteem
A heart so warm of a busy honeybee

This gentle man named Sir Richard
Weathering life's storm
With eight decades of stories and an army man for glory

Etched on his face

A tapestry of memories Time cannot erase.

In the twilight of days His legacy blooms

For Sir Richard, the laughter, the joy

Of his loved ones sitting in this room

Today they honor, celebrate and toast

The Man, The Legend, The Legacy

At The King's Throne sits...His Majesty, Sir Richard Bloom

Never Knew What I Had

By Riccardo Marini – 2024
Never knew what I had till I said goodbye
Always searching for a strand of grass
Greener on the other side.

Never meant to break your heart
Never meant to tear us apart

Like a lost little boy, I started to stray
Took our dreams and tossed them away

Like lost lotto tickets torn in half
Or diminished confetti swept in the trash

Always stepping out to a new dance
Searching for another hot romance

I, an addicted love gambler
Roaming the streets for another stranger
I took your precious trust
Traded for a moment of lust

A thief in the dark stealing your faith
Crushing your hopes
Never making your pain dissipate

I grew tiresome of telling lies
I began to notice tears in your eyes

Today is tomorrow that fearfully arrived
I stand alone you're no longer by my side

The gentle whispers are silent in my ear
Your indelible touch vacant, it's all so clear

All the love you offered

I exchanged

For a night out and a cold glass of beer

The flickering candle blew out in your heart

Like a shadow slowly fading to black

The seasons have passed but your essence survives

In my mature years I have realized

Never knew what I had till I said goodbye

Searching for a strand of grass

Greener on the other side

Greener on the other side

My Couch, My Friend

By Riccardo Marini – 2024 -
Inspired by Eddie Cordiano

It keeps giving
It cares how I'm feeling
Sick, happy or crying
It embraces me even when bleeding

Socializing, fantasying or just chilling
Always there
24 hours per day awaiting my arrival

It asks for nothing in return
Just me sitting, movie watching
Till I'm dreaming
My Couch, my best friend

During all seasons
Cozy during winter chills
Relaxing thru hot summer days
Watching fall leaves ever changing

Rain droplets dripping, dripping
Snowflakes falling
Day dreaming, cloud watching

Nighttime cocktails
Thinking, reflecting of life choices
Friends, family, children

Work and a lot more
A morning cup of joe
A quick snack
A pre-bedtime snore

My couch, my friend
you're inspirational
and so desirable

The minute I open the door
I see you, naked and all alone
It's where I belong

I hear your whisper
Quietly begging
Come lay down

You and I, Till the very end
We can conquer the world
My old friend

Virginia's Room

by Riccardo Marini

I spend my moments in time in a home named
Jeanette Where I fell in love with a special person I
met

Her eyes are brilliant blue
She sparkles having a flare for fashion
I stare while my mind burns with passion

Her phrases, her thoughts,
With little effort she speaks so eloquently
Her charm, her expressions, I listen so endlessly

Her gestures, her walk, it all seems like a ballroom
dance
How I stay watching, like a puppy in a trance

Speechless I quiver like a bashful child
I wonder do I have the presence to make her smile

Each day I sit next to her so close
I hear her beating heart, like a beautiful symphony
Little she knows she whirls my mind-up in a state of tragedy

I wish for a sunset beach walk, holding her hand so fine
So, I could whisper in her ear
Lady you're my fantasy please be mine

Then one day I said "Hi hon, I'm home"
Little did I know I had entered Virginia's dome

I cannot help falling in love with this person I met
Intelligent and pretty like a flowerbed

I think of her all day and dream of her by starlight
Wondering will I ever make love to her throughout the night

A million sparkling diamonds
Reflected by sunshine out at sea
It is the inspiration I feel when she's so close to me

I feel I'm in a state of tranquility
Soaring like an eagle high above
She will always have a place in my soul for eternity

One day, I'll look back and say
"How fortunate I am to know her in this special way"

This angel walked into my life and stole my heart
My life feels complete; I can't bear to be apart.

"Lovers In the Dark"

by Riccardo Marini

We made love all night
Till the sun came up
We were lovers in the dark

You knew all along
I was married and you were not

You didn't seem to care
For all in love was fair

The first time we met
We both agreed
No broken promises
No regrets

Our first date at La 'cote D'argent
Your favorite French restaurant
We shared our hearts
Over Crepes Suzettes

It was a special moment
Strange how we met
By midnight we were in heaven

We strolled in the park
Sat on a bench to reminisce
Picked forget me knots
Like two lovers in the dark

We traveled about
Never went one day without
When we made love
The stars came out

We took a romantic trip to Frisco
Made love on the beach in Sausalito
Walked in a blizzard in Reno

We both drank Dewars on the rocks
Danced all night at "Land of OZ"
Like two lovers in the dark
Like two lovers in the dark

"Mellisa"

by Riccardo Marini

You can find her on a floating vessel
A mermaid in disguise
She likes to shop at the mall
For stiletto heels for your eyes

She stands six feet tall
Wears sensual designer clothes
With an awesome smile
That would float your boat

She can enter a room
And the party starts
Her looks and words are always smart

She can swim in a pool
Or sit on the rocks
Sipping her favorite libation
Margarita on ice

She hates lies
She hates deceit
She wears elegant graffiti on her sleeve

She can dance, she can swim
She can be nice
She can pour-on the romance
Like a melting candle of a witch's trance

She swims with Joe
A handsome guy with an electrical flow
That can drink and party

Like a pirate afloat
She's slick like a mermaid at sea
When she departs, the party stops
As she sprinkles her angelic lust
An invitation you can't refuse
To her next appearance
Dawn to dust

A vision of the sea
She makes this world
A better place for all to be
Her sparkle is etched
In every diamond
On the ocean's crest.

"MAJID"

by Riccardo Marini – 2023

He's calm and in control
He possesses a gentle soul As
he traveled the world

At times selling
At times engineering
At times pondering

He's committed to family
He's committed to driving
He's committed to living

Each day he arises at dawn
Each night he arrives at dusk
With a goal of all tasks
Completed a must

Day in and day out
In all types of weather
He always carries a smile
He has walked a 1000 miles

He negotiates contractor's terms
Reviews plans and submittals
Change orders and deliverables

Performs inspections
Design documents for breakfast
Deployment and mobilization

RFIs and Permits
Audits and meetings
Always with a professional greeting

He's focused on details
His life a blueprint
To build the best, a person can be

We share ideas, we share expectations
As he works alongside me
With integrity and meaning
My new friend and mentor "Majid"

"Gone My Choir Song"

by Riccardo Marini – 2016

I'm knots and knots of twisted nerves
Waves of tears overflow my river

I dream of her each minute
Her satin skin, once I touched
Sleepless lonely nights begin and begin

Happiness jettisoned
The future darkened
On moment's notice by
A ferocious coyote winds

Her Choir Song now transformed
Her lyrics silenced
Her ageless fluorescence lit my nights
A beggared twilight I forlorn

Her cote-azure eyes faded

Her lips asleep as I weep, weep, weep

Lost in a grey whirling gust

Twisted tumbleweed and blinding dust

Twirl, Twirl the turnstile of fears

Now I lay buried in layers of emptiness cheer

Gone her wonder, the beauty she brings

As I am only empty space

Breathing silently in a lifeless thing

Rise Above

By Riccardo Marini – 2015

I spent my days sliding on the distant tenuous hills of
worry
Approaching closer to a daily path of
Unsurmountable mountains I was forced to climb.

Far away from the fields of peaceful glory I envisioned
in my mind I
struggled not to slip on the rocks' ledge
Many times, I faulted and fell into the valley of
despair eagerly waiting below.

Never had a moment of heartfelt rest
Battered, bruised and bloodied, I resumed my
seemingly endless quest.

Every morning, I awoke to be faced with the cold winds of life
The rains bitterly stung my face like spikes

Fear was my morning ray of light
it peered thru the tempestuous clouds of doubt
It affected my very being,

Like a thief in the night, robbing my spirit, raping my soul.
Others around enjoyed their sunny life,

I inwardly suffered in silence with every blow
I choose the path of naivety and trust

I had reached the crossroads of no return.
I had traveled terrains and destinations unknown.

Neither a compass, nor training or defense
I could not stand still, I forged ahead.

The struggles were not anew
Many were set by trail blazers I foolishly followed.

Not a sip of water in my empty flask
Walking barefoot on shattered glass

Never a restful night's sleep
Often awakened by broken promises

Vanished dreams in thin air
Scarily wondering how I would fare

At times I could have had some respite
But like an unknown mystical force
I surrendered myself to assist some other I placed before me.

Cashing in would wait for a later date.
Foolishly watched my assets slip from my grip.

Mis-calculated the time I had,
Cost of compound interest for bad decisions once made.

Silent hidden enemies lay in wait
An ambush at dark was my fate

My resolve to weather the storms of time
The droughts of failure, the famine of success
Poor emotionally vested acquaintances once called family and friends

All with time heals the wounds
The scars may still be seen I, and felt n my heart
A remembrance of the past

The peaceful fields of glory envisioned now I stand
I see the sunrise I eagerly love and befriend.
I Rise Above. I Rise Above.

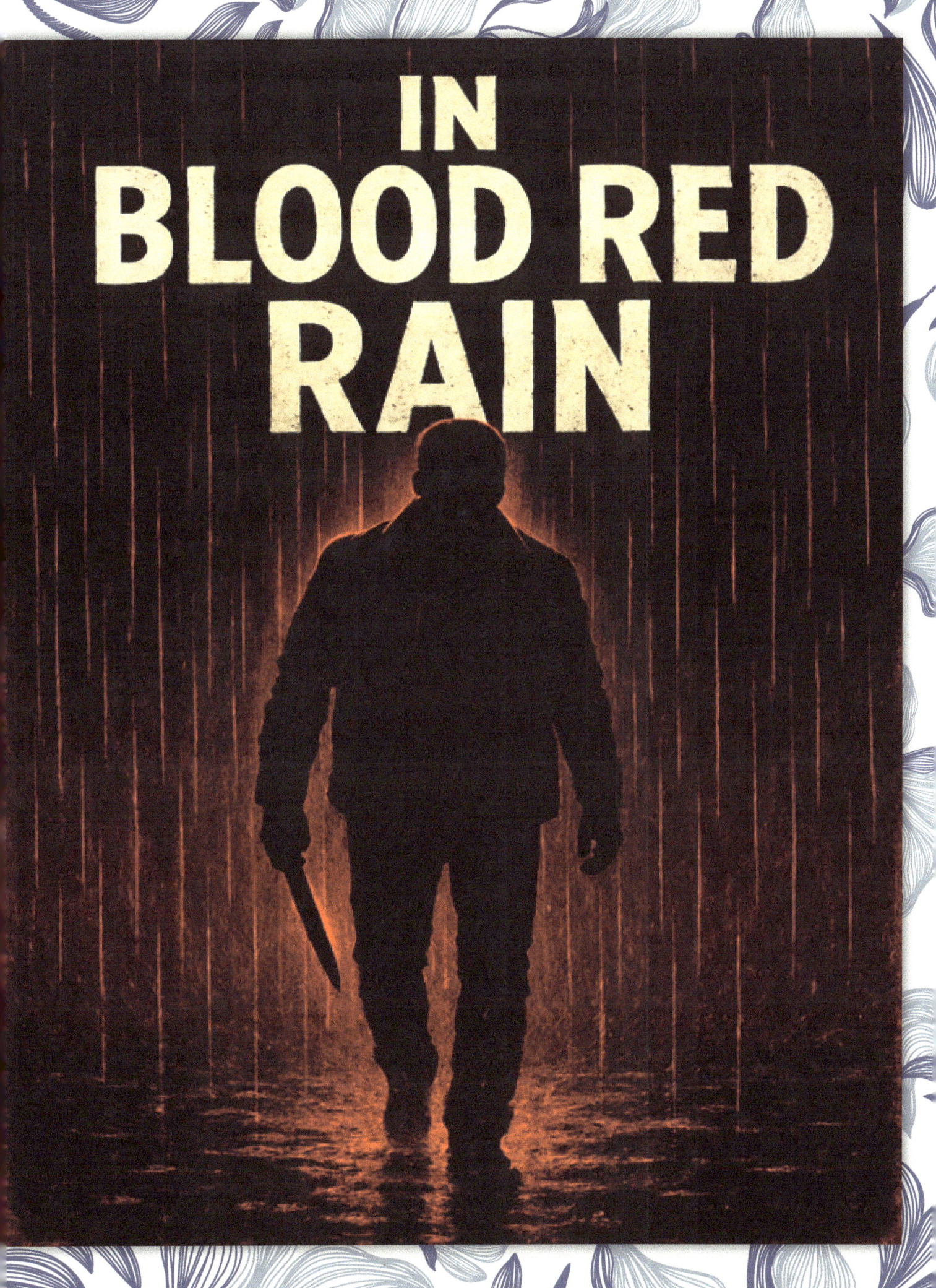

The Blood Red Rain

By Riccardo Marini -2016

Lonely dark nights, knights that wander
Cunning beasts that pace and ponder

Dripping sweat and drooling saliva
Quenching their thirst of blood, they hunger

Gladiators with make-shift swords
Cheering spectators wanting more

Ranting cuttings! cuttings! Conquistadors
Hour by hour a list is drawn

Who shall commit mortal sin once more?
A forgotten mothers lost first born

The revolving door spits two men
To fight a battle nobody wins, nobody mourns

Barron and bright the sun burns
At the Bare Hill Prison, inmate's scorn

Beyond, beyond, some seagulls fly
Landing on a rusted, tin roof top, near by

Peering through wired windows with grimaced grin
A feud of minds begins
A collision spawn

Danger boils and tempers flare
The anger, anger, twister spins

The crazed malaise settles in
Throughout the beige metal bins

At half past midnight
Under snow white linen

The red stain razor's pain begins
You can hear the swish of slashing
Through thick and thin

The sparks of spears,
the thud of thunder

The spikes of sinister,
Pierce one-to-other,
With torrential hatred
One day to another

The blood red rain floods within
It pours, pours and pours

The Bare Hill River overflows

A slice of life

Some got to know

And some seagulls watched in woe.

"The Shadow's Dance"

By Riccardo Marini – 2020

No one rings the bell
No one calls
No cards are in the mail

The fireplace still burning
A Shadow is hiding and lurking
For a Shadow's Dance

Wearing a dark mask
No one's around walking
Yet the Shadow has a task
For a Shadow's Dance

I stare at the walls
With slanted picture frames
Of stained forgotten photographs
Once called friends

Begging for them to jump out
Drink, laugh and hang out once again

I don't want the Shadow to know
How fragile and forgotten I am

He watches every step I make
I pray he trips, forgets or makes a mistake

I wish I could flee
I'm too old, frail and it's too late

The old coffee table with scratches and nicks
In the corner an ancient book still sits
With unfilled prescriptions I risked

I read all night while the Shadow laughs
None reveal remedies curing my faith
Or my fears which now walk in my steps

I'm tired and weak and I clearly see
Through closed blinds of morning sunshine
Filled with dusty streaks

Piercing through a quiet empty room
The Shadow silhouette joyfully greets
Would you like to dance?

He lives day by night
With sinister grin
Of whom he chooses
The next dance victim

He's in the news
He's in my living room
With no conscience
He's ready to dance

Another day passes
Another chance awaits
For the Shadow to celebrate

He counts the numbers
He gladly takes
He doesn't discriminate

Young and old,
Weak and strong
They now all belong
Waiting online for their turn

Another night in fearful trance
The fireplace flickers
While the Shadow's dance

I see a glimpse of an amber glistening
Like a spotlight focusing
On the invitation it reads

Good evening my friend
I'm recruiting once again
For the Shadow's Scorn Dance

The club tuition is free
Your enrollment begins
And I'm your host
The infamous Covid-19
Hahahahahahahaha.

"Four Clovers We Not"

By Riccardo Marini – 2020

Our skins have whelked
Our soul's un-wealed
Our future betrayed
With broken promises once made

Our tears can't abate
The road of indifference we take
We wonder what awaits
We wonder our fates

Gone for now the coral reefs
The dust unsettled beneath our feet
An angry earth in grief
An angry earth in grief

The veil of beauty now feigned
The fountain of youth poisoned in vain
All in our sands of time
Only a few grains remain

Spinning, spinning faster than slow
The Northern lights no longer aglow
The oceans overflow
The magnetic field reversed

The sun scorches and burns, scorches and burns
The hurricane winds of time
They blow, they blow
Till nothing stays the same
Someone is changing our game

The wars still fight for the infamous government fools
The bullets still fly, the guns still rule
But the dead that are found
Are the children in our schools

The landscape changed, we await, we await
Our words define new meaning in our times

What once meant this, now means that
We can't seem to syncopate

The sidewalk crack, now a drug
My mother's pot, now a smoke
A bottle of coke, now a snort
We give birth to new words that hurt, that hurt
Nika and Covid, Sars and Mers
Al-Qaida and cli-fi galore
Death at doorsteps DuJour
We become the next dinosaurs

Our wrinkles and scars reflect
The custody and oversight
Of another stepchild in neglect
The abuse few will forget

Overwhelmed with mind fatigue
Widgets and gadgets all we see
But not our indiscretions
Against you or me

Higgledy-piggledy
Biggety we be
Four Clovers we not
Four Clovers we not.

Shattered Glass

By Riccardo Marini – 2021

She stood before me one day
Sensual, tall and beautiful
Greeting me; "Hi I'm Rachel"

An angel model with a smile
Large Godiva Chocolate eyes
Long lashes signaling playful

I was transfixed only heard every other word
I trembled, trembled and trembled

I tried to keep my composure
She on the other hand
Confidant, exuberant

I wanted to know her
I couldn't put my finger
on what I sensed

Knowing one day I would be discarded
Like torn confetti left over on a
New Year's Eve bandstand floor

Like many before me
That walked thru her door

I knew then, we would never stay friends
And no one would care for her more
No one would care for her more

Young, experienced on the surface
Inside... fragile, blurred visions
With patterns of indifference

I wanted to wave a DNA wand
Guide her on a healing pathway
If granted only time beyond
Would she understand

And no one would care for her more
She after all was a hard find
Perhaps one of a kind

I knew we would never stay friends
Cause one day I too would stand
On her Shattered Glass mind.

"A Man, A Bud Can and A Setting Sun"

By Riccardo Marini 2023

In the twilight of his years with Budweiser in hand
With stories to be told he quietly stands

A carpenter by trade, he shaped his world
With crafted tales of the road.

But his life on land soon got old
And to the Sea is where his passions would be.

With a boat, bait & pole and little frills
His weathered soul tells the tales
Down his long memory road

With each sip cold and chilled
His sandy hourglass of time
Reflects the ocean's fishing thrills

His hands calloused and body bruised
from his hard work, a craftsman builder
in shadows he'd lurk.

Beneath the gruff exterior lay the heart of a pirate
A fisherman's spirit, resilient with one goal
To rape, pilferage and drink to be bold.

At times he lived on the road, like a nomad of old
His stories, like treasures, forever unfold

A boat, his companion, fished the waters wide
Through the highs and lows, with the changing tides.

Direct in his words, no room for disguise
He'll tell you how he feels, never shy
Couldn't care less about your feelings
Or if he made you cry

He's an 80-year symphony of laughter and wise
In each day echoes the past
A lifetime of memories to outlast.

With eyes that sparkle, like stars in the night
He's a testament to living, a beacon of light
An 80-year saga, a tale well spun
Of a Man, A Bud Can and a Setting Sun.

"Mitch The Miracle Man"

By Riccardo Marini – 2023

Known as a super caregiver man
Does he know how much it means?
Does anyone consider being his fan?

The lives he touches
The sacrifices he makes
Making someone feel better
Every chance he can

At times at his expense
He puts up with rudeness
At times it turns to crudeness

But he keeps on giving
At times he displaces his pain
So, some other can reap the gain

He can prepare a meal supreme.
He's detailed and spotlessly clean
He possesses not a bone of mean

A good shopper indeed
At times a barback tender
Or anyone that needs a helping hand

A hard worker and contributor
A fighter when provoked
A giver not a taker is his plan

He enjoys a good Italian lunch
Some Cake Chef Cookies
And raspberry Linzer tarts

He's all about kindness
Someone to count on
Someone to befriend

He's all about kindness
Someone to count on
Someone to befriend

"A Dream Named Nigina"

By Richard Marini, 2020

A beacon of bright, intelligent, light
Like a star sparkling in the heavens of time
With streaks of golden hair kissed of sunshine

She wears silky
With threads of shyness woven in kindness
At times you can see a flicker of loneliness

She stands out in a crowd
With arms open, like a sunflower child
Embracing us with her charm

A sensual silhouette
With an unmatched wit
Slick like a cat

She speaks in a tone of a soft whisper
She flashes a gentle grin
One look and you don't know where to begin

Her lashes gently brush her beauty
Painted on a fragile porcelain doll
With shades of pastel pretty
She possesses the charm to stimulate
With a heart to reciprocate
With a mind of intricate

A soul tempered with lace and delicate
Wearing a halo of an angel
Stirring within a bit of devil

All in the fanciest style
Prancing thru life like a dancing ballerina
With a magical flair and a stunning figure
Serving you a Dream Named Nigina.

All I Wanted Was Love to Feel

By Riccardo Marini – 2017

My heart shattered
by your poison spears
My soul drowned
in an ocean of fears

You were so
selfish, always about you
You never cared about me

You just had not a clu
But if the foot was on
the other shoe

I'm glad in a way
you're no longer her

But if the foot was on
the other shoe
You would cry out,
till the moon turned blue

I'm glad in a way you're no longer here
Perhaps I can mend my life and heal

All I wanted was respect to hear
All I wanted was love, to feel

"All I Wanted Was Love to Feel"

By Riccardo Marini – 2017

My heart shattered by your poison spears
My soul drowned in an ocean of fears

I cried a river of tear
I'm glad in a way you're no longer here

You were so selfish, always about you
You never cared about me

You just had not a clue
But if the foot was on the other shoe
You would cry out, till the moon turned blue

The drama, the hurt, the sting
I lived with all your flings

Staying out late, going on dates
Coming home late, betrayal was our fate

We created a child
You failed to provide
You didn't care, not for a little while
I'm glad in a way you're no longer here
Perhaps I can mend my life and heal

All I wanted was respect to hear
All I wanted was love, to feel.

A Rat in a Closet

by Riccardo Marini – 2024 - "Dedicated to Chico"

Thrown into this world, like a rat in a closet,
Searching for sustenance
Trapped and void of windfall profits.

Who's to blame, my parents or me?
I've done all I can, yet I struggle to see.

Sometimes I falter, not grasping the cost,
Of choices I've made, the paths that I've lost.

I could have been more, I could have been grand,
I could have been this, I could have been that
I had a talent, but fear held back my trigger,
Buried deep in the sand.

Yet it's not too late, I've still got the fire,
Just need one last chance to rise and aspire.

I can navigate darkness, avoid of light
Take off my boxing gloves
I'll plan through the night.

With every last ounce of strength I possess,
I'll claw my way up,
Through my shoulder's weight
Fatigue and stress.

From where I now stand,
There's only one way—
Straight up to the summit,

Where hope lights the day.
I will never return
This trip is a one way

To join the world and give what I can
As less have given more
And more have given less

I will change my world

Thanks to Virginia my prophet

Cause I never will return

Like a rat in a closet.

www.ingramcontent.com/pod-product-compliance
Lightning Source LLC
Chambersburg PA
CBHW041145120626
46547CB00020B/3124